Armour
Christy Ducker

Smith/Doorstop Books

Published 2011 by
Smith/Doorstop Books
The Poetry Business
Bank Street Arts
32-40 Bank Street
Sheffield S1 2DS

ISBN 978-1-906613-36-5
Typeset by Utter
Printed by People for Print, Sheffield

Acknowledgements

Thanks to the editors of the following, in which some of
these poems first appeared: *Envoi*, *Magma*, *The Reader* and
The Wolf. 'Skeletons' was first published in the anthology *Lit*
(NWN, 2009). I am grateful to New Writing North for their
help and support. Thanks also to Linda France, Cynthia
Fuller, Bill Herbert, Jenny Larby and Bruce Woodcock, and a
special thank you to my family.

Smith/Doorstop Books are a member of Inpress:
www.inpressbooks.co.uk. Distributed by Central Books Ltd.,
99 Wallis Road, London E9 5LN

The Poetry Business gratefully acknowledges the help of
Arts Council England.

Armour is a winner of the Poetry Business Competition,
2010/11, judged by Simon Armitage

Contents

Getting Rid of the Aphids

Instead of a way out
she finds a sack.

It arrives at the greenhouse
each Thursday.

Once set down,
the sack fidgets

until she loosens it
and pours out

one kilo of ladybirds.

For a moment
she sees only

stunned treasure
hissing to a standstill

but soon
the ladybirds fly
whirring.

Hunting, they stud
the soft hurt
of tomato stems.

At night
they fall from her clothes –
brilliant

even in darkness.

Skeletons

At what point do we say *There. It stops there*
and decide to forgive the man whose family
once shipped slaves, or the woman whose father
upset a nation with rumours and guns?

Perhaps it's the point at which I would say
my husband's family used to duck witches
but when I nearly drown, off Galway Bay
one night, he swims for me and helps me breathe.

Perhaps it's the point at which I would say
yes it's a beautiful ivory box
of the heirloom his mother displays
detached from the blood of its carving out.

Perhaps it's the point at which I might learn
to love the present flesh that softens bone.

The Working Woman's Right Breast is Not Amused

Yes, I tried to be patient and fair
when she told me about her *career,*
forgetting that I can express myself too
in the strongest of possible terms.

But Number One child, she rushed him away
so he barely remembers my name
and Number Two is already dispatched
down to *Kidz in a Tizz with Nadine.*

So I thought I might spook her a bit
with a hint at some salt in my works,
which is why I lie here teat up
for inspection in hospital greens.

As we stare at my gubbins on screen,
my nodes come up pouting like mouths
that are movie star blooming and clear –
she concedes that she must be *run down*

so with luck, a bit later, she'll take me
out rowing and dabble a hand
down my stoup, while I ask for more kids
who I secretly hope will be hungry, and male (and twins).

Entering the Country

The soles of your feet haven't touched the ground
but still you're asked to *wait in line* with all

the wall-eyed grown-ups. I hold you aloft
so you can see how other babies globe

their cheeks at you, as you begin to breach
the hush that cramps us in this hall. You light

on children's sounds, until you've hawked
your English *da da da* for Xhosan clicks

that dovetail with Punjabi *bah* then pitch
into Malayan *neeyang*s before a flit

towards the ceiling. Airline staff worry
our papers. New flights arrive and depart.

Small wonder then, that two days on
as we cut bread and lay out plates, you stun

us all when down the runway of your tongue
your first word comes. *Aeroplane*. Its wings

fuelled by a lifetime, it circles our lunch
three times, then zooms out the door through a cloud

of mosquitoes. We watch it recede,
feeling the tremor of journeys begun.

Descent

It was my kick that did it, made you shout
Hooligan! made me clatter the beer can
along the Quayside and into the past –
to *Hoolihan*, great great grandad Molloy

who bowls at me on the wheels of his name
allowing a glimpse of his beery face
as he drives off the bank of the Liffey.
With a grasp on the reins of his dray

he slants into flight immortal,
coat tails parting on the whole performance.
For an instant, his weight confounds the air
before he descends to a crapule of mud

and although I try to dodge his downfall
my great great grandsons will bear his brunt.

Nest

Move earth sip by sip
up to the eaves.
Secure walls
with articulated spit.
Dispense with foundations.
Believe. Bowl
eggs into place.
Avoid brooding.

Sit tight
incubate flight
sleep weather-wise.
Neb your chicks
then launch them.

Migrate. Return.

Journey

You always broke my fall
While I was running down
My love, my life, my all.
I ran into a Dane

While I was running down
The Finnish one who smoked.
I ran into a Dane
He liked the way I spoke.

The Finnish one who smoked
Was very good in bed,
He liked the way I spoke
About the Scot I said

Was very good in bed
(He's not as good as you).
About the Scot I said
It's time for him to go

(He's not as good as you).
I wanted you to stay
It's time for him to go
You held me straightaway.

I wanted you to stay
You always broke my fall
You held me straightaway,
My love, my life, my all.

Deer

Too often roadkill or sprung space,
our deer survive and come back north
pressing themselves to the house for warmth.
They're close enough to show their lice
teeming through fur that looks combed.
They'll bolden soon and scruff our fence
with moult, a herd of hoist-bellies
up for scraps they lick from my palms
on the day you venture out again,
all bristle and stink, warming to spring
with skin that's slackened on grief.
Gods from off the mountain, you'll say
in your grandiose way and stoop
while I kiss you in firm belief.

Elizabeth Sheds her Inhibitions

I left them in a teal blue box
on a shelf above the lawnmower.
I locked the door on them quite firmly,
discarding the key down a well.

I then dug up the other keys
I had buried once out of fear.
Those were the keys I later left
in the lap of the homeless girl.

After snapping all the heads
from my husband's despicable roses,
I watered the weeds I love
and fed the crops to the cows.

I didn't eat, not a jot until dusk
when I served up four cold cuts.
I passed the port to the right and across
the space where the silver once sat.

By dark, I was riding bareback
on the horse I have seldom had time for.
Together we galloped all over the lines
laid down by neighbourhood dispute.

Lastly, I rode to see the young people
who queue in few clothes outside night clubs.
It was then I came across you officer.
And what a fine, fine officer you are.

The Life of Facts

1111

The midwife claps and counts
her blessings, fingers the caul
from the baby's head. She swipes
a cloth around the child to fish
for scraps of luck. She knows
the cloth will sell in strips
to seamen at the harbour
who'll wear it near their skin
to keep the world from running out.

*

1515

Holding my newborn in my hands,
I think of the wrong I've done.
My family will abandon me for dead,
when Upik tells them what he saw.
He's made *Inukshuk* of me, stitched
my hair in a bag of bones that vanished
through a sealhole. If I'm to live,
I'll need to go where sea ice bends,
where footprints melt around the brink.

*

2058

You want a boy so tick *Male*.
The doctor rigs pipettes
beside a window that's been rainy
now for months. You come to
Eyes, tick *Blue: no squint*. A tremor
rolls in from the coast, again
the building wavers. You check the pen
at *Feelings* where the column falls
away beyond the table's edge.

Fortune

You will wake up to snow outside
and drink, without chipping at ice.
You will eat meat you did not kill.

Even though you are a woman,
you will read a letter, twice.

You will speak the same language
as a girl you admire
and you'll do so without meeting.

You'll get rust in a cut
but it will not kill you.

You will make a child
with a man from abroad,
while looking at stars that have names.

You will stand
on a round earth that spins.

Your horizons will always be level.

Armour

I'd rather be a lobster,
in pre-op, not knowing
whether I'll fail
on the surgeon's table.

The lobster has plans:

he can tear away
a limb in battle,
scrinch off home
and await new growth.

I've no such armour

only this ape's design
that frees my arms
to hold onto people
who'll shield my heart.

Madness, to a lobster

who keeps his head down
the shape of him claiming
that meat appears
that fight happens

miles from the ape

with her brain a fruit
in the treetops seeding
chatter and quips
while her fingers crack lice.

I wake up later

stitched into myself,
embracing the nurses
embracing you
making light

Three Dances

A Lesson in Quickstep for Strangers

In the aftermath,
we've been learning to fly
        this stranger I married
        and I. The secret, I find,
                is in short steps
                and following
while clearing the way.
I would dance
        twice as quick as time
        to free his heavy feet,
                to skirt dead ends
                and *keep it light*.
Our teacher's instructions
are for men's feet but mine
        do the opposite
        to make it work.
                With feathersteps,
                I try to lift
the weight of our difference.
I tiptoe. His hand flutters my back
        to make a new wing.
        He flaps
                at the edge
                of letting go.

Each window
is open tonight, *just in case*
        we pull it off, an airy dance
        for flat stones who trust
                each other
                enough
to balance and fly true
to skim the lagoon
        of a ballroom floor
        with a skip, skip

                and skip, skip and
                skip, skip, turn

*

Turn

Practice shoes fall to bits by the end,
fold in on themselves, stinkhorn-like.
Gold heels, built to *wow*, spend the night
bagged. Oxblood brogues trip the light
fantastique, then sulk in tissue, boxed.
Neat black pumps come to rest
in dressy-up chests and the

                            reason

                                      is

this: that your feet want to go, cut a rug,
throw the floor out the door, and then
plant themselves tuber toes down in the loam.
They want to dib in to where dancing came
first, to a time when a foot could go gleaning
at night, to a time when your feet
would spin blood into children or wheat.

*

The Triple Mambo

Let's dance! he said
No chance, she said,
>> *I'd rather*
kiss, she said
like this and bopped
>> her fingers
down his spine,
then frisked his hairline
>> with her tongue
like this, she said,
like this. He said
>> he'd rather
stand apart
and watch her start
>> to want him,
watch her breasts buzz
through the fuzz of
>> That Black Top.
So watch me then,
she said, *you watch*,
>> her hips rolled
out of reach.
Just watch me pout
>> *your name*, she said,
her lips
jujubes for him
>> to eat.
I want your taste
he said, *come here*,

23

his short steps
stretched out long.
She touched his hand
                    It's time now,
Love, to do zig
zags, to do that
            cha
                        cha
            cha

24

And

suddenly you are here
and I am astonished
by the way you smell of bloody bread
and the way you already decide
to place a webbed fist here,
to slow-wink a newt's eye there.
I am astonished that you are purple.

And now I know glee
at the indignant heaving bellows of your belly,
your self-startled arms flung wide proclaiming
your tiny chimp gums.

And I watch to see time
measured by your face,
crane as you push each new word through glottal air.
I thrill because you're not like me
but you and young and other.

One Who Adds

When you were born, we became similar,
your dad and I. We started to smile at
the same time because you were lovelier
than all the *good* boys. We never doubted
you'd be a different fruit, not when you ran
at dad in the blazing heat and called him
Bright-and-Orange. After that, you began
to say your dad and the sun were the same.
Or when you hopped towards me in the dark –
I turned you to the light and watched you shoot
across the yard in ecstasy. Suchlike
I'd not seen, least of all in a spacesuit.
I can hardly even remember us
from the days before you set us both loose.

Nit Nurse

Mention God and I think of the nit nurse
who sailed on a cloud of pink mohair
above the cheese polish floor of the Hall
where we herded to her, right from sermons
on love *Almighty*, to be in the fold
of her dough breasts, her tickle and talcum.

A part of me nuzzles there still, thrilled
by the way her fingers knew my earbones,
the way she tilted my head to the light
as if she were seeking a hallmark
before she would pause and register
the sum of my hairs, each one unharmed.

I sometimes wonder where she went,
if she basks in flamingo sunsets, abroad
while I hum and hah at the chemist's
over how to shrive my children's hair,
knowing she'd want me to home in
with a toothcomb rather than slick potions.

How Mackie Did the Drowning, Plashetts

To begin, he moved into her kitchen,
slouched on a chair while she fried up *hinnies*.
He brought in pine cones, dubbin, swamped
her smell of cotton-scorch and Bibles.
Every night, to dry their tongues, he hung his boots
from bedrails near the stove. He slaked himself
on her, before he told her how he'd dammed
her river, how a flood would come. He stayed
a while, until the first wave reached the hearth,
until it climbed the panelling. He left
for higher ground, the day the waters floated
Jesus off the wall, back turned forever.

That's when he edged up Belling Hill, to watch
her rooftop disappear, her chimney brim with water.
The lake he made weighed four years.
Some days he thought he'd drink the lot
to fill the space inside him. Instead, he cast stones.

Plashetts – the drowned village beneath Kielder Reservoir, Northumberland

Footing

Before I became a wall, I was spread out as one big puzzle.
I was pulled from the burn and the field, and I was all in pieces.
I had always been there, before I was pulled, but not in this order.
Now that I stand between fields, I have ended an endless squabble.
Now I have bumpy shoulders, I am built to trip up the sheep.
I am built with strong sides, I am built out of forces, I balance.
Beneath my skin, I am full of patterns, I am full of hearting.
My footing is firm and it's broad: my footing is old as the fells.

Asylum Seeker

I came here in a coffin without handles.
Bruises healed. I began to dig gardens.
In Algiers, I was an archivist of bones.

The Talking Island

And you my love were here for years
so long that lichen frizzed the stones
you settled here to cloister thought
exalting in my tall skies

Our time was full like your Book
lit by every colour I gave
the life you spent here listening
to my birds my seas and sootfall

When you left I tried to come too
by spooring myself to your clothes
though your long white legs scissored away
and you cloaked yourself in elsewhere

Your followers crowd ashore now
to search for you in me
but find instead an ark of land
weathering flood for those who stay

Grace Darling Learns to Count

Brownsman Island, 1821

1 is a lighthouse, a person standing,
a finger raised, commanding *ssshhh* –
the course of a gannet's dive.

2 is a neb-nose duck out paddling,
a plane for wood or a girdling pan,
it's the cold squat of yesterday's iron.

3 is a guillemot tilting gales
4 is a sail in the Fairway tacking
hoving a cargo of more numbers:

5 will hook on fast to memory,
8 will moor with a rope twist
round and around the docking horns

but 7 is harder, like the cut
in your sister's lip
only the Mainland mentions.

6 and 9 keep troubling you –
two whelks in a rock pool tumbling
away from any sense of up

but 10 is your mother at the spinning wheel;
it's you learning the world
whose numbers come to learn you.